CUZ I LOVE YOU

Words and Music by LIZZO,
SAMUEL HARRIS, CASEY HARRIS,
ADAM LEVIN and RUSSELL FLYNN

LIZZO
CUZ I LOVE YOU

PIANO
VOCAL
GUITAR

ISBN: 978-1-5400-6744-9

Visit Hal Leonard Online at
www.halleonard.com

Contact us:
Hal Leonard
7777 West Bluemound Road
Milwaukee, WI 53213
Email: info@halleonard.com

In Europe, contact:
Hal Leonard Europe Limited
42 Wigmore Street
Marylebone, London, W1U 2RN
Email: info@halleonardeurope.com

In Australia, contact:
Hal Leonard Australia Pty. Ltd.
4 Lentara Court
Cheltenham, Victoria, 3192 Australia
Email: info@halleonard.com.au

LIKE A GIRL

Words and Music by LIZZO,
SEAN DOUGLAS and WARREN OAK FELDER

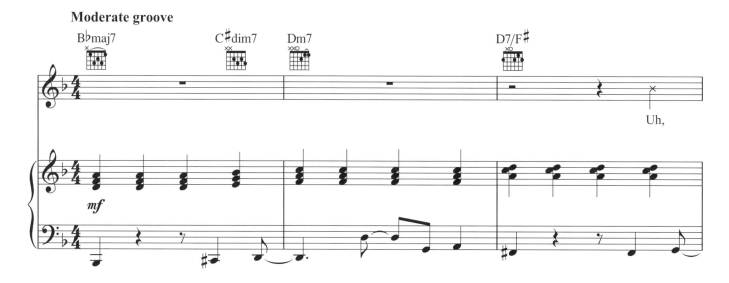

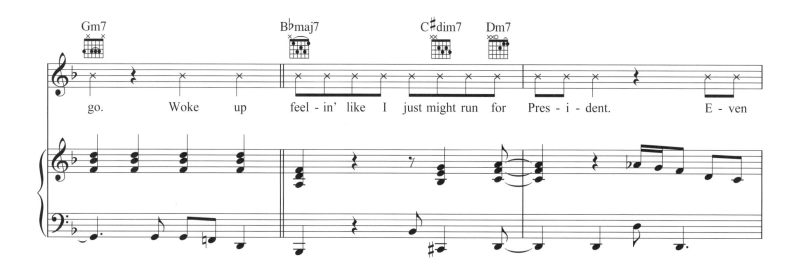

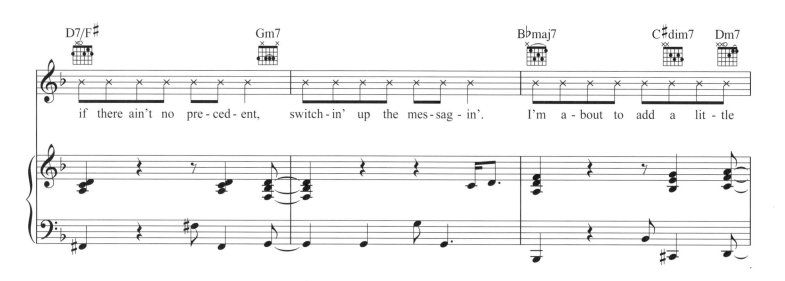

JEROME

Words and Music by LIZZO,
SAMUEL HARRIS, CASEY HARRIS,
and ADAM LEVIN

JUICE

Words and Music by LIZZO,
THERON MAKIEL THOMAS, ERIC FREDERIC,
SEAN SMALL and SAM SUMSER

SOULMATE

Words and Music by LIZZO,
SEAN DOUGLAS and WARREN OAK FELDER

love fi-n'lly hap-pens when you by your-self. __ So if you by your-self, then go and buy your-self __ an-oth-er

round from the bot-tle on the high-er shelf. 'Cause I'm __ my own

Look up in the mir-ror like, "Damn, she the (I'm the

one. __ I'm the one. __ I'm the
one." __

one, _____ the one.) Look up in the mir-ror like, "Damn, she the

one, one, one, one, one, one, one." Like, "Damn, she the one, one, one, one.

That bitch in the mir-ror like "Yeah, I'm in love, in love."

That bitch in the mir-ror like, "Yeah, I'm in love, love, love, love,

Yeah, I'm __ my own soul - mate No, I'm __ nev - er
(Look up in the mir-ror like, "Damn, she the one.")

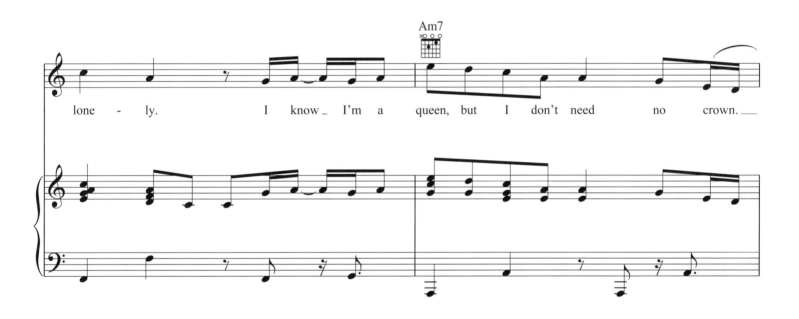

lone - ly. I know __ I'm a queen, but I don't need no crown. __

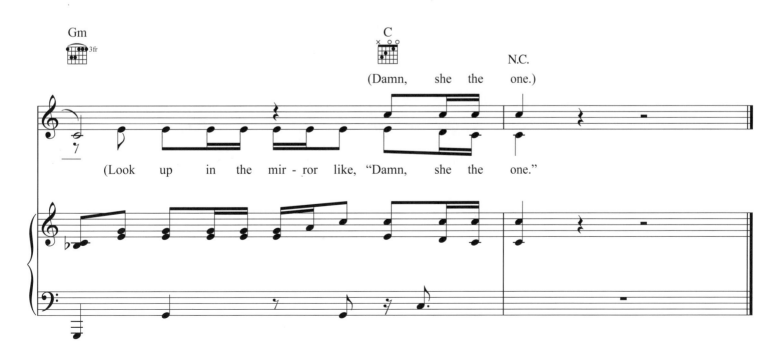

(Damn, she the one.)

(Look up in the mir - ror like, "Damn, she the one."

CRYBABY

Words and Music by LIZZO,
ERIC FREDERIC, NATE MERCEREAU
and CHARLES HINSHAW

Pull this car o- ver, babe. _

Don't pre- tend like you _ don't know. _ A

lot of girls _ have time _ for this shit. Hon- est- ly, I don't.

TEMPO

Words and Music by LIZZO,
THERON MAKIEL THOMAS, ANTONIO CUNA,
MELISSA A. ELLIOTT, DAN FARBER,
ERIC FREDERIC, RAYMOND SCOTT
and ERIC TOBIAS WINCORN

Freely

(Spoken): I've been waiting for this one. . . . turn it up!

Moderately

Slow songs, _ they for skin-ny hoes. Can't move all of this here to one of those. I'm a

thick bitch, _ I need tem-po. Fuck it up to the tem-po.

*Recorded a half step lower.

EXACTLY HOW I FEEL

Words and Music by LIZZO,
THERON MAKIEL THOMAS and MICHAEL SABATH

With a groove

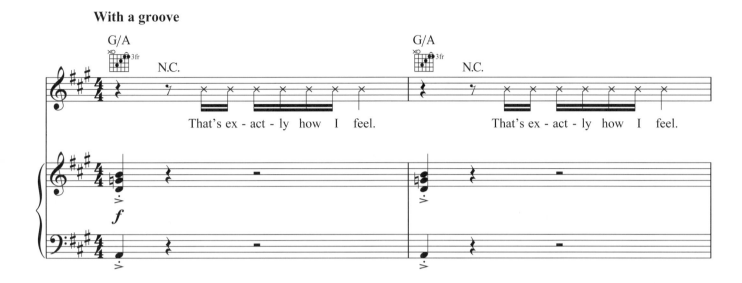

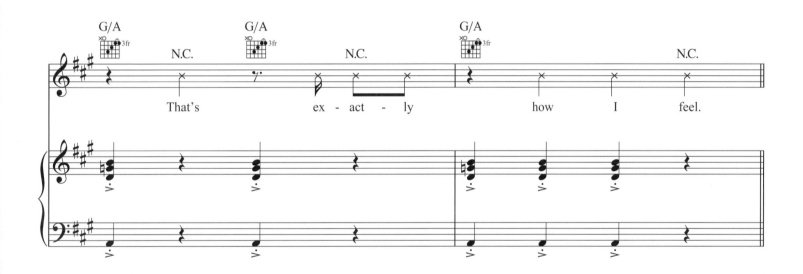

BETTER IN COLOR

Words and Music by LIZZO,
TREVOR DAVID BROWN, WILLIAM ZAIR SIMMONS,
WARREN FELDER and MICHAEL POLLACK

HEAVEN HELP ME

Words and Music by LIZZO,
SAMUEL HARRIS, CASEY HARRIS,
and ADAM LEVIN

TRUTH HURTS

Words and Music by LIZZO,
ERIC FREDERIC, JEESE ST. JOHN GELLER
and STEVEN CHEUNG

LINGERIE

Words and Music by LIZZO,
THERON MAKIEL THOMAS, ERIC FREDERIC
and NATE MERCEREAU

Slow groove

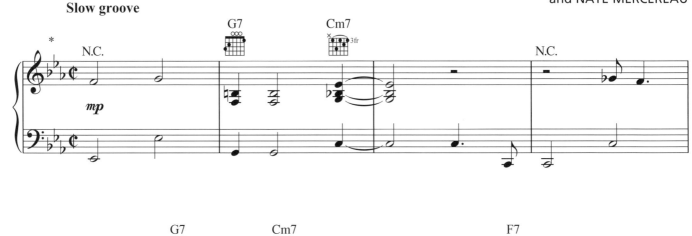

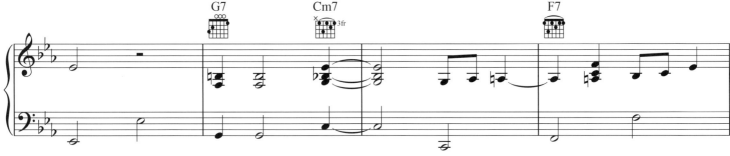

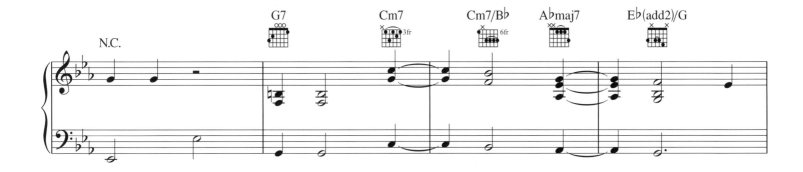

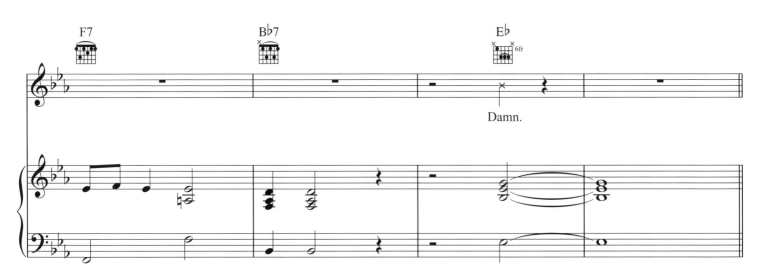

Damn.

Recorded a whole step higher.

Vocal written an octave higher than sung

* *Vocal written at pitch*

Vocal written an octave higher than sung.

More Songbooks from Your Favorite Artists

JONAS BROTHERS – HAPPINESS BEGINS

14 songs from the 2019 album marking the triumphant return of this trio of brothers who started out as Disney Channel stars. Includes: Comeback • Cool • Don't Throw It Away • Every Single Time • Happy When I'm Sad • Hesitate • I Believe • Love Her • Only Human • Rollercoaster • Strangers • Sucker • Trust • Used to Be.

00300594 Piano/Vocal/Guitar $19.99

P!NK – HURTS 2B HUMAN

This 2019 album from pop diva Pink topped the Billboard® 200 charts led by the single "Walk Me Home." Our matching songbook includes piano/vocal/guitar arrangements of this song and a dozen more: Can We Pretend • Circle Game • Courage • Happy • (Hey Why) Miss You Sometime • Hurts 2B Human • Hustle • The Last Song of Your Life • Love Me Anyway • My Attic • 90 Days • We Could Have It All.

00295728 Piano/Vocal/Guitar $19.99

BILLIE EILISH – WHEN WE ALL FALL ASLEEP, WHERE DO WE GO?

This debut studio album by this teenage newcomer to the music scene reaching the top of the Billboard® 200 album charts. Our matching folio features 13 tracks: All the Good Girls Go to Hell • Bad Guy • Bury a Friend • 8 • Goodbye • I Love You • ilomilo • Listen Before I Go • My Strange Addiction • When the Party's Over • Wish You Were Gay • Xanny • You Should See Me in a Crown.

00295684 Piano/Vocal/Guitar $19.99

ARIANA GRANDE – THANK U, NEXT

This 2019 album, released on the heels of Grande's popular 2018 release, *Sweetener*, topped the Billboard® 200 album charts. Our piano/vocal/guitar songbook features the hit title track, the followup blockbuster "7 Rings" plus 10 more: Bad Idea • Bloodline • Break up with Your Girlfriend, I'm Bored • Fake Smile • Ghostin • Imagine • In My Head • Make Up • NASA • Needy.

00292769 Piano/Vocal/Guitar $19.99

DUA LIPA

17 songs from the self-titled album by the 2019 GRAMMY Award® winner for Best New Artist, Dua Lipa. Includes: Bad Together • Be the One • Begging • Blow Your Mind (Mwah) • Dreams • Garden • Genesis • Homesick • Hotter Than Hell • IDGAF • Last Dance • Lost in Your Light • New Love • New Rules • No Goodbyes • Room 4 Two • Thinking 'Bout You.

00278038 Piano/Vocal/Guitar $17.99

SHAWN MENDES

Mendes' 2018 self-titled album debuted at the top of the U.S. and his native Canadian Billboard® album charts. Our matching folio features all 14 tracks arranged for piano, voice and guitar: Because I Had You • Fallin' All in You • In My Blood • Like to Be You • Lost in Japan • Mutual • Nervous • Particular Taste • Perfectly Wrong • Queen • When You're Ready, I'm Waiting • Where Were You in the Morning? • Why • Youth.

00279536 Piano/Vocal/Guitar $17.99

TAYLOR SWIFT – LOVER

Matching folio to Taylor's latest blockbuster, record-breaking, chart-topping album featuring 18 songs including: The Archer • Cruel Summer • I Think He Knows • London Boy • Lover • The Man • Me! • Paper Rings • You Need to Calm Down • and many more!

00322682 Piano/Vocal/Guitar $19.99

DEAN LEWIS – A PLACE WE KNEW

A dozen tracks from the debut album by this rising Australian pop star in arrangements for piano, voice and guitar. Includes: Be Alright • Chemicals • Don't Hold Me • For the Last Time • Half a Man • Hold of Me • A Place We Knew • 7 Minutes • Stay Awake • Straight Back Down • Time to Go • Waves.

00295529 Piano/Vocal/Guitar $19.99

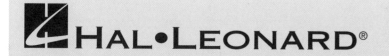

For a complete listing of the products we have available, visit us online at **www.halleonard.com**

Contents, prices, and availability subject to change without notice.